WORDSKILL 1

Christopher Walker

A Piccolo Original
Piccolo Books

A note to parents

Wordskill 1 is designed for children between the ages of 7-9 years. This age range is of course, approximate and should not be taken as a rigid guideline as children's reading and writing skills develop at very different rates.

This book has been designed to complement and reinforce much of the language work taught at school, but it uses a more informal approach. The stories, rhymes and riddles and puzzle-type activities have been selected to increase and enrich your child's vocabulary, encourage accurate spelling and stimulate enjoyment in reading. The main aim of the book is to get children to **think** about words, their meanings and how they are used and spelt. Though the stories and rhymes are meant to be enjoyed for their own sake, they are also used as the basis for a variety of language puzzles and activities.

Wordskill encourages children to put pen to paper and work on their own at their own pace. Occasionally they may call for help. When this happens, you can help out in the following ways:

☆ Read the poem or story with the child.
☆ Help with difficult words and spellings.
☆ Don't give your child the answer. Rather, attempt by your questions to get the child to seek correct solutions. Give plenty of praise and encouragement.

It is very important that the work is taken in short stages. The activities are there to be enjoyed. When they stop being fun, it is time for a rest and a change. Therefore encourage your child to work in short bursts. Don't keep him/her at it until it becomes a chore.

Your involvement in your child's language development is of the greatest importance, and although most of the activities can be tackled by the child alone, we hope that the book will provide opportunities for discussion between you. Enjoy the book **together**: the greater the enjoyment, the more your child will relax and gain confidence, and the more he or she is likely to learn from it.

All answers can be found on pages 31 and 32.

Rhyming Riddles

How good are you at riddles?
Here's your chance to find out.

In each rhyme below, one word is missing.
That word is the answer to the riddle.
Write your answers in pencil.

1. It has no mouth, you know,
   Nor does it have a jaw,
   Yet it has teeth — all in a row,

   What is it? It's a 1 _____ .

2. When on the trampoline you go,
   And in the air you climb,
   What season is it? Do you know?

   The answer is 2 _____ .

3. Your uncle has a sister, May,
   She is not your aunt, that's clear.
   Yet she's related to you in some way,
   Just how, please let me hear.
   She can't be your cousin, as you know.

   So she must be your 3 _____ .
   Isn't that so?

4. As Mr Jones went down the lane,
   A skeleton passed by,
   He said 'Today it's going to rain.'
   So Mr Jones asked, 'Why?'
   'So you can't be sure,' said Jones.
   'Oh! Yes I can,' came the reply,

   'I can feel it in my 4 _____ .'

Rhyming pairs

Name the objects in the pictures.
Write the names which rhyme on the lines.

Kite and light
star and jar
well and bell
book and hook
____ and ____
____ and ____
____ and ____

The odd one out is _____ .

Mixed up Maisie on the farm

Maisie went to stay at her uncle's farm. One day a jet plane zoomed over. It was very low and made a terrific noise. It frightened all the animals. Maisie wrote a letter home telling about it. This is what she wrote.

Dear Dum and Mad,
                Tojet a flew day over. It noise a terrific made. All the frightened were animals. You never din heard a such. The dogs were quacking. The pigs were neighing. The cows were clucking. The ducks were grunting. The hens were barking. The horses were mooing. Noise a what!
    After an about quiet all was hour again.
        Loves of lots
        Maisie XX

As you can see, Maisie got all mixed up.
Can you rewrite the letter so that it makes sense?
Don't change the order of the sentences.

The Minotaur

Long ago the people of Athens went to war with Crete. Minos, king of Crete, won the war. He forced his enemies to keep an awful promise. Every year he made them send to him, fourteen young men and women. The seven most handsome youths were chosen. With them went the seven most beautiful girls. In Crete they were put into a maze. No one ever came out of it alive. Once inside they were hopelessly lost.

The maze was the home of the Minotaur. This monster had the body of a huge man. His head was that of a bull. With his cruel horns he tossed the victims against the stone walls of the maze. Then he ate their broken bodies. Each year this was the fate of the youths and girls sent from Athens.

The King of Athens had a son named Theseus. One year the prince begged to be sent as one of the youths to Crete. His father agreed and the prince boarded the ship. The sail was black, the colour of mourning. No one expected to see the prince again.

Theseus was a brave fighter. He hoped to kill the Minotaur. He promised that if he did, he would come home in a ship with a white sail.

When they got to Crete the victims were brought before King Minos. Theseus begged to be the first to go into the maze. The king agreed.

'Tomorrow,' he said, 'you will go into the maze. You will spend your last night in prison.'

The prince was led away to his cell. He did not know that the daughter of King Minos had fallen in love with him. In the night she came to his cell. She gave him a sword and a ball of string.

At daybreak the guards put the prince in the maze. He waited till the guards went back to the king. He tied one end of the string to a rock. Then he went in search of the monster. He laid out the string as he went.

Soon he was hopelessly lost. The string was almost used up. Then as he turned a corner, he found the monster waiting for him. Time and again the bull-man charged. Each time the prince dodged nimbly aside. Then the prince slipped. The monster saw his chance and charged again. At the last minute the prince rolled out of his path. The monster could not stop. He hit the wall with a sickening thud. His horns shattered against the rock. Theseus leapt in. Dragging back the monster's head, he stabbed it in the throat. The monster sagged and lay dead at his feet. The prince rolled up the string and followed it safely out of the maze.

King Minos was told what the prince had done. 'He is a brave man,' said the king. 'He shall go free and all his companions with him. Make their ship ready to sail home.'

The prince and his friends set sail. But they forgot to change the sail for a white one. High on the cliffs the prince's father waited for the ship to come into view. When the black sail appeared the king thought his son was dead. He threw himself off the cliffs and was drowned in the sea far below.

All the answers to this puzzle are words in the story 'The Minotaur'.

Use a pencil. You may need to rub out.

Clues across

1. friends
3. son of a king
4. pleaded
6. secured
7. labyrinth
8. threw
10. sight
12. opportunity
13. monarch

Clues down

2. sank
3. gaol
4. got on
5. pulling
9. pass
11. go by boat

Forgetful Freddie

Freddie always forgets when to write capital letters.
Today I told him two rules about them.
Here they are.
1 **The first letter in a sentence is a capital.**
2 **The first letter in people's names is a capital.**

Then I read some sentences to him. I asked him to write them down. This is what he wrote.

1 we went to mary's house today.

   _____

2 today is dick's birthday.

   Today is Dick's birthday! ✓

3 did you know that janet is ill?

   Did you know that Janet is ill? ✓

4 my best friend is peter.

   My best friend is Peter.

5 would you like some sweets, anne?

   _____

6 pat jones is a good runner.

   _____

You see that Freddie forgot his capitals again. There is a space under each of Freddie's sentences.
Rewrite each sentence in the space below it. You should write two capital letters in each sentence.

Name the game

In which games are these things used?

1 bat
2 _____
3 _____
4 _____
5 _____
6 _____
7 _____
8 _____
9 _____
10 _____

Creature chain

START

ANTIGERAMAGPIEARWIGULLOBSTERACCOONEWTOADUCKIDOGOATURTLEAGLEARTHWORMACKERELADYBIRDRAGON

FINISH

Look at the letter chain.
In it are the names of twenty creatures.
All the names overlap.
Write them in **order** below.

1 _____	2 _____	3 _____
4 _____	5 _____	6 _____
7 _____	8 _____	9 _____
10 _____	11 _____	12 _____
13 _____	14 _____	15 _____
16 _____	17 _____	18 _____
19 _____	20 _____	

DIRTY GERTIE

How good are you at making rhymes?
Let's find out.

In this poem are twenty spaces.
One word is missing from each space.
First read the poem. Then think of the best word to put in each space.
Lastly, write your words in the spaces.
The first one is done for you.

This is the tale of a girl named Gertie,

You never saw a girl so 1 _dirty_ .

The very thought of being clean,

Would make young Gertie turn bright 2 _____ .

And as for soap, that was a word,

You'd think that she had never 3 _____ .

Her mother wondered why her daughter,

Should be so terrified of 4 _____ .

Whenever she was put in it,

The girl was sure to throw a 5 _____ .

So Gertie always went to bed,

Covered in dirt from feet to 6 _____ .

She'd never had a bath last year,

Till one day, coming from her 7 _____ ,

They saw a plant had taken root.

Her mother gave a frightened 8 _____ .

'Just look,' she said, 'She's grown a flower,

We'd better get her in the 9 _____ .

'Come on,' she yelled to her husband Bert,
'We must get rid of all that 10 _____ .'
Well, Dirty Gertie fought like mad,
To keep away her Mum and 11 _____ .
But, after what they both had seen,
They meant to get their daughter 12 _____ .
They ran the bath. Then pushed her in.
Their daughter made an awful 13 _____ .
The more they scrubbed, the more she'd roar,
They scrubbed until her skin was 14 _____ .
They kept on scrubbing half the night,
Till Gertie's skin was shining 15 _____ .
In fact, it was at half-past three
When Gertie's Mum said 'Oh dear 16 _____ .
'I think,' she said, 'we'd better stop.'
We've scrubbed away our Gertie's 17 _____ .'
'We have indeed,' said Bert. 'Look there
We've scrubbed off every single 18 _____ .'
So do be warned, you little girls.
If you should want to keep your 19 _____ ,
Keep clean, it's foolish to be dirty.
Remember what became of 20 _____ .

Step by step

Name the objects in the pictures.
Then fit the names in the spaces.
Five words go across.
Five words go down.
Use pencil. You may need to rub out.

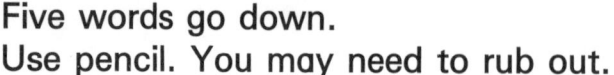

Silly spellings

Look at these silly spellings.
They are all animals' names.
The letters are in the wrong order.
Can you put them in the right order?

1. A R T
2. G O D
3. L I N O
4. A L E S
5. R E E D
6. H E A R
7. F L O W
8. T O A S T
9. S H O R E
10. A M L E C
11. R E T O T
12. T A R B I B
13. K E Y N O D
14. S E E L A W
15. R E D B A G
16. R E D P O A L
17. H E N T R A P
18. R A G I L L O
19. T E N A P O L E
20. T H E P L A N E

_____
_____
_____
_____
_____
_____
_____
_____
_____
_____
_____
_____
_____
_____
_____
_____
_____
_____
_____
_____

Mr Jinnocky and the squeaking stair

Mr Jinnocky is very old. I'd say he's about a thousand. He spends nearly all his time in his garden. He only goes in to eat and sleep. The lawn is always like velvet. He cuts it with nail scissors then smooths it down with a nail file. The flowers are great! The roses are as big as footballs and they climb all over the house.

Mrs Jinnocky is old too. She is not keen on gardens. She likes her house from the inside. Everything is bright and shiny and smells of furniture polish. She is very proud of her house and is always nagging Mr Jinnocky to do the repairs that she cannot manage herself. She is particularly annoyed at having a squeaking stair.

This stair makes the most amazing noise. If you put one foot on it, it sounds like a hundred dying cats. If you put two feet on it, you'd think ten coachloads of witches were after you.

Every night Mrs Jinnocky tells Mr Jinnocky to mend the squeaking stair and every night he takes no notice of her.

Well, one day, Mrs Jinnocky got fed up. She told Mr Jinnocky, 'I'm going to visit my old mother (who must be a million years old). I'll be gone for about a week. You had better mend that stair while I'm away.'

Mr Jinnocky was glad to have a bit of peace for a while. On his way to bed, he jumped three times on the squeaking stair with glee.

In the middle of the night Basher Bates arrived. His picture was in every police station. It said on the picture "£10,000 REWARD". Nobody could catch him because he was the biggest burglar in Britain. And the nastiest!

Basher Bates broke into Mr Jinnocky's house. 'They'll keep their money upstairs,' he thought. So he went upstairs without a sound until he came to the squeaking stair. Basher Bates was very, very big and so the noise he made on the stairs was very, very loud. It sounded as if a thousand policemen were shouting, screaming and using their whistles. Basher nearly leapt out of his skin. He fell over backwards and rolled down the stairs. His head hit each step, thud, thud, all the way down until he lay unconscious at the bottom.

Mr Jinnocky got up and saw Basher Bates on the floor. He got a big net that he was going to use for his sweet peas and wrapped it all round the burglar. Then he got the clothes line and tied him up.

When Mrs Jinnocky watched the News on the television, she couldn't believe her eyes. There was Mr Jinnocky clutching a cheque for £10,000 and telling how he had caught Basher Bates single-handed.

'This man came in the middle of the night,' he said. 'I punched him in the jaw. Down he went. I tied him up and then I called for the police.'

Mrs Jinnocky thought, 'I never knew my husband was so tough. I'd better not nag him again.' And she never did.

And Mr Jinnocky never mended that squeaking stair. As far as I know it's squeaking still.

As for Basher Bates, he was never the same again. When he read the headlines: 'Pensioner knocks out giant burglar', he was so ashamed he gave up burgling for good.

All the answers to this puzzle are words in the story 'Mr Jinnocky and the Squeaking Stair'.

Clues across

1. angry
5. approximately
6. astonishing
9. jumped
11. great merriment
12. noise

Clues down

1. came
2. almost
3. scold
4. obtained
7. pleased
8. repair
10. also

NEW WORDS FOR OLD

Name the object in each picture.
Use the letters in each name to make a new word.

1 _____ nuisance
2 _____ to cut the corn
3 _____ to listen to
4 _____ the beach
5 _____ not tall or high
6 _____ a baby horse
7 _____ to puff out air
8 _____ noise made by sheep
9 _____ tree which grows dates
10 _____ a number

Make a word

Put one letter in each empty square to make a word.
All these words start with CAN.

#										a clue
1	C	A	N	e						a stick
2	C	A	N	a	l					a man-made waterway
3	C	A	N	d	y					sweets
4	C	A	N	o	e					a light narrow boat
5	C	A	N	a	r	y				a yellow bird
6	C	A	N	d	l	e				a light made of wax
7	C	A	N	n	o	n				a big gun
8	C	A	N							an easy run
9	C	A	N	c	e	l				to stop, postpone
10	C	A	N	T	E	E	N			a place where meals are made

All these words start with MAR.

11	M	A	R	K						a stain or scratch
12	M	A	R	E						a female horse
13	M	A	R	C	H					to walk smartly
14	M	A	R	R	Y					to wed
15	M	A	R	S	H					a swamp or bog
16	M	A	R	B	L	E				a small glass ball
17	M	A	R	G	I	N				edge, border
18	M	A	R	I	G	O	L	D		a yellow flower
19	M	A	R	G	A	R	I	N	E	used instead of butter
20	M	A	R	M	A	L	A	D	E	orange jam

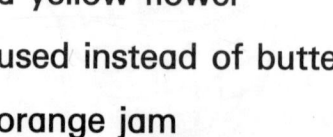

MAGIC E

The letter 'u' has two main sounds.
It can be silent like the 'u' in run.
It can be long like the 'u' in perfume.

In 'cute' the 'e' is a magic 'e'.
It makes the 'u' call out its name.
(Its name is 'you').
The 'e' has no sound.

Now look at the pictures below.
Under each picture are two spellings.
Only one spelling is correct.
Put a ring around the correct spelling.

1 duk   duke   2 club   clube   3 mul   mule

4 cub   cube   5 costum   costume   6 tub   tube

7 tun   tune   8 tub   tube   9 cub   cube

A tall story

One day Pat and Fred were walking into town. It was a long walk. 'To pass the time why don't we tell each other tall stories?' said Fred.

'A good idea,' Pat agreed.

'To make it more fun,' suggested Fred, 'I will pay you five pounds if you can make me say that I don't believe your story and you pay me five pounds if you don't believe mine.'

'OK,' said Pat.

Fred was sure that he would win. He thought it would be easy to trick Pat. 'I will start,' he said. 'Once an elephant flew down and landed in my back garden. Do you believe that, Pat?'

'Surely,' said Pat. 'Elephants have big ears. They could use them as wings.'

Fred went on. 'Then he knocked on my back door and asked me the way to Heathrow Airport. Do you believe that, Pat?'

'Surely,' said Pat. 'Elephants have mouths. They could use them to talk.'

'The elephant landed at Heathrow Airport and two thousand passengers climbed on his back. Do you believe that, Pat?'

'Surely,' said Pat, 'Elephants are big. The first passengers could sit on his back. Then others could get on their backs and so on.'

Fred went on. 'The elephant took off. At ten thousand feet he stalled. He dropped like a huge stone and went straight through the centre of the Earth and landed in Australia. Do you believe that, Pat?'

'Surely everyone knows that Australia is the other side of the world.'

Fred saw that Pat was not as simple as he thought. He could not be tricked. Fred gave up.

'Right,' said Pat, 'Yours was a good story and it was all true. I know because the elephant's wife wrote me a letter. She asked me to get her husband back from Australia. So I got a rope and lowered it down the hole. The elephant tied the rope around his middle and I pulled him back. Do you believe that, Fred?'

'Surely,' said Fred, 'everyone knows how strong you are Pat.'
Pat went on, 'The elephant's wife was so pleased to see her husband again that she gave me a five pound note. Do you believe me, Fred?'
'Surely,' said Fred, 'and five pounds does not seem much for such a heavy job.'
'That's what you said at the time,' said Pat.
'Did I?', said Fred in surprise.
'You did. Don't you believe me?' asked Pat.
'Oh, I do,' said Fred hastily.
'Well you ought to,' said Pat, 'you were right there with me.'
'Yes, I remember now, I was with you, of course,' said Fred.

'You were,' said Pat, 'I remember you saying you had no money so I lent you the money the elephant paid me, . . . and by the way, I would like my five pounds back right now.'

Poor Fred saw that he had been tricked. He could not say he had not borrowed the money, that would be to call Pat a liar and would cost him five pounds. If he said he had borrowed it he would have to pay it back. Either way he had lost five pounds.

All the answers to this puzzle are words in the story 'A Tall Story'.
Use a pencil. You may need to rub out.

Clues across

1. begin
3. astonishment
5. task
6. large
8. plan
12. very big
13. deceive
14. alighted
15. short for 'Patrick'

Clues down

2. considered
3. remarked
4. certain
7. delighted
9. You catch a plane here
10. tale
11. easy

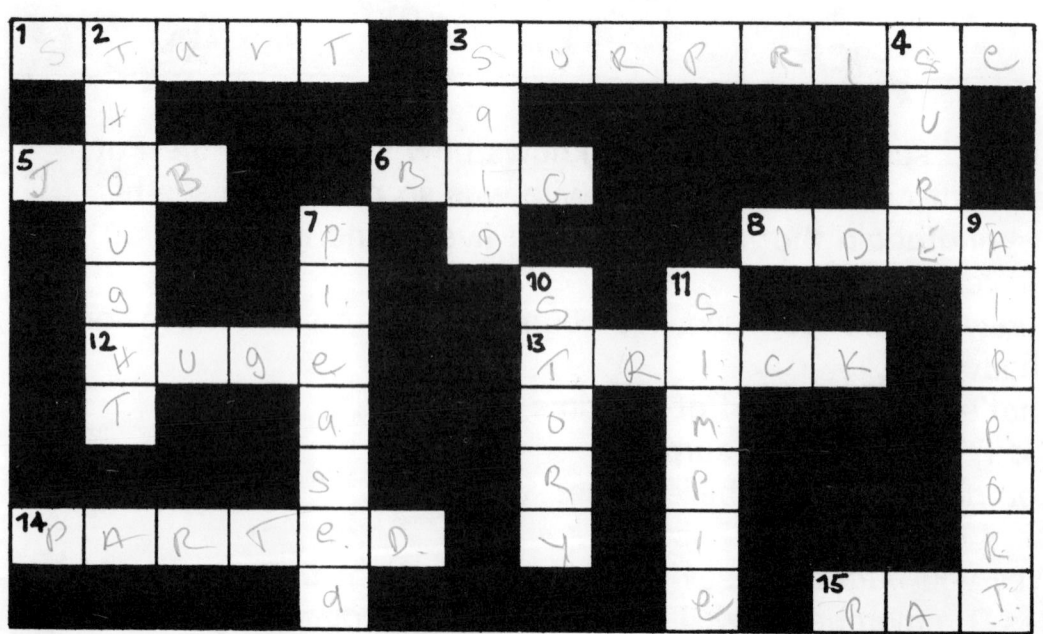

Hidden numbers

Have you got sharp eyes? Find out with this puzzle.
There is a number hidden in each sentence below.
First find the numbers. Next underline them.
Then write each one in its answer space.
The first one is done for you.

1. Do not g<u>o ne</u>ar the cat — it may scratch you.
   Answer <u>one</u>

2. I felt hot yesterday but I feel even hotter today.
   Answer two

3. The lake is choked with reeds — it is not safe to swim there.
   Answer three

4. We must buy a new tent — ours lets water in.
   Answer ten

5. Don't be afraid of the dog — it won't bite you.
   Answer _____

6. The bank robber had a gun in each hand.
   Answer _____

7. Panther, our kitten is missing — we must find it.
   Answer _____

8. On sports day Mary won the most girls' events.
   Answer _____

9. I'll call and see you this afternoon if I've time.
   Answer _____

10. Pat went yachting on the lake yesterday.
    Answer _____

Rhyming riddles

How good are you at riddles?
Here's your chance to find out.

In each poem below, one word is missing.
That word is the answer to the riddle.
Write your answers in pencil.

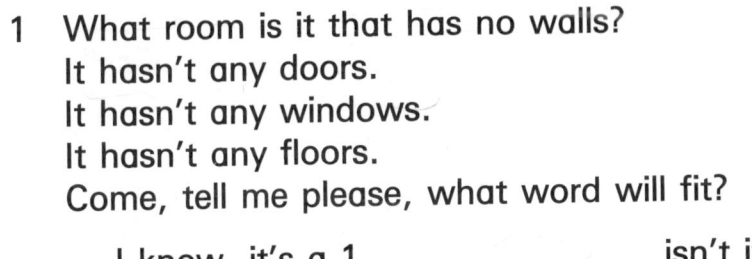

1. What room is it that has no walls?
   It hasn't any doors.
   It hasn't any windows.
   It hasn't any floors.
   Come, tell me please, what word will fit?

   — I know, it's a 1 _____ , isn't it?

2. They locked me in a room
   With a piano in it.
   I soon got out of there,
   It took me just one minute.
   I played the piano, do you see,

   Until I found the proper 2 __Key__ .

3. Though it has hands, it has no feet,
   And so it cannot walk.
   It has a face but cannot see,
   It tells but cannot talk.
   — Oh that's an easy one for me,

   The thing's a 3 _____ , don't you agree?

4. Tom lost his dog in the woods one day,
   He really was upset.
   His friend came walking by that way,
   He said, 'Tom, do not fret.
   We'll find your dog. Just wait and see.'
   Tom said, 'What, in the dark?'
   His friend said, 'Yes. Put your ear to a tree

   and listen to the 4 _____ .'

The memory game

Get a sheet of paper.
Number down the margin from 1-15.
Study the pictures for two minutes.
Think which things go together.
There are **five families** with **three things** in each.
Then close the book.

Write down the names of all the things you can remember.

Spell backwards

Name the object in each picture.
Then write each one backwards.
You should make a new word each time.
The first one is done for you.

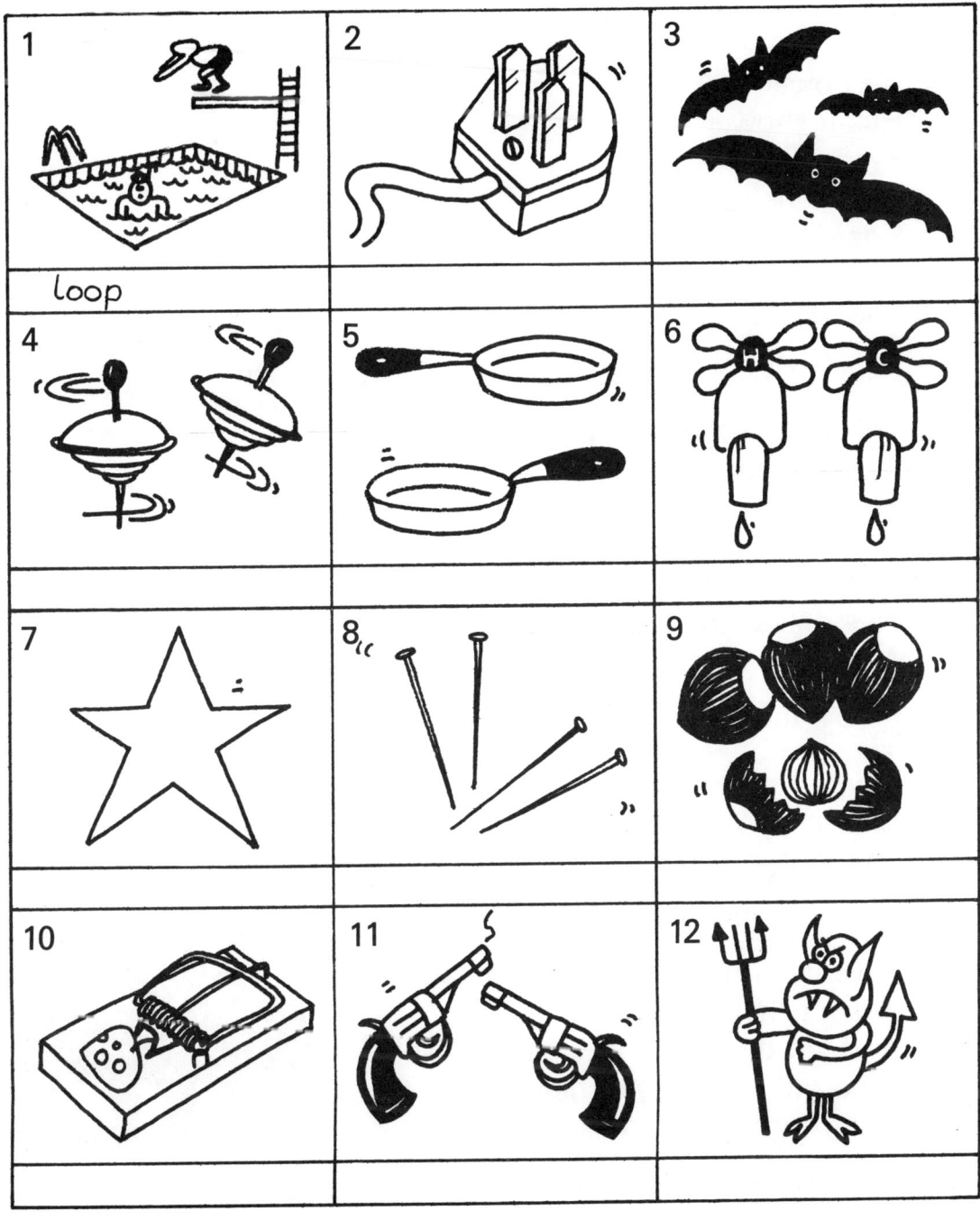

Rhyming riddles

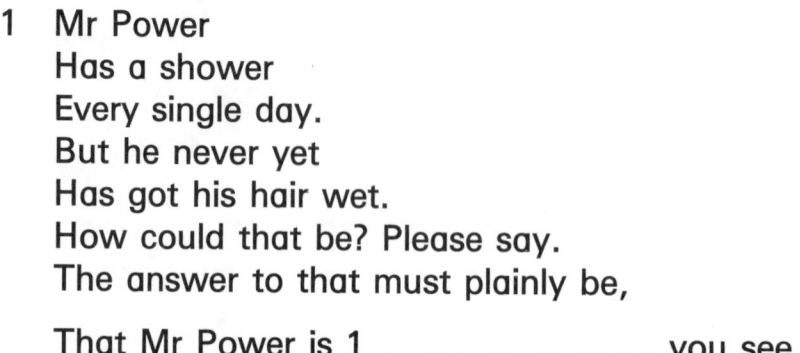

How good are you at riddles?
Here's your chance to find out.

In each poem below, one word is missing.
That word is the answer to the riddle.
Write your answers in pencil.

1 Mr Power
   Has a shower
   Every single day.
   But he never yet
   Has got his hair wet.
   How could that be? Please say.
   The answer to that must plainly be,

   That Mr Power is 1 _____ , you see.

2 This object goes from side to side
   And sometimes up and down.
   It even travels nationwide
   And goes through every town.
   Now here's the strangest thing of all —
   This object cannot move at all.
   And now, before your brains explode,

   Here's the answer — it's a 4 _____ .

3 Never trust anyone in bed,
   Even if they're dying.
   The reason is, I've heard it said,

   They'll probably be 3 _____ .

4 Seventeen men under one umbrella.
   Wasn't that a sight?
   And yet there wasn't a single feller,
   Who got wet all that night.
   Oh! That is easy to explain.

   You see, there wasn't any 2 _____ .

Answers

Page 3

(1) a saw, (2) springtime, (3) Mum, (4) bones

Page 4

goat — coat
jar — star
bell — well
arrow — barrow
lock — sock
book — hook
kite — light

The odd one out is 'jug'.

Page 5

Dear Mum and Dad,

Today a jet flew over. It made a terrific noise. All the animals were frightened. You never heard such a din. The dogs were barking. The pigs were grunting. The cows were mooing. The ducks were quacking. The hens were clucking. The horses were neighing. What a noise! After about an hour all was quiet again.

Lots of love,

Page 8

Across
(1) companions
(3) prince
(4) begged
(6) tied
(7) maze
(8) tossed
(10) view
(12) chance
(13) king

Down
(2) sagged
(3) prison
(4) boarded
(5) dragging
(9) spend
(11) sail

Page 9

1 We went to Mary's house today.
2 Today is Dick's birthday.
3 Did you know that Janet is ill?
4 My best friend is Peter.
5 Would you like some sweets, Anne?
6 Pat Jones is a good runner.

Page 10

(1) cricket, (2) tennis, (3) darts, (4) hockey, (5) golf, (6) dominoes, (7) chess, (8) rugby, (9) badminton, (10) table tennis

Page 11

ANT TIGER RAM MAGPIE EARWIG
GULL LOBSTER RACCOON NEWT TOAD
DUCK KID DOG GOAT TURTLE EAGLE
EARTHWORM MACKEREL LADYBIRD
DRAGON

Page 12/13

(2) green, (3) heard, (4) water, (5) fit, (6) head, (7) ear, (8) hoot, (9) shower, (10) dirt, (11) Dad, (12) clean, (13) din, (14) sore, (15) bright, (16) me, (17) mop, (18) hair, (19) curls, (20) Gertie

Page 14

(1) HARE (2) EGG (3) GOAT (4) TIE (5) EAR
(6) RAKE (7) ELF (8) FROG (9) GUITAR
(10) RAINBOW

Page 15

(1) RAT (2) DOG (3) LION (4) SEAL (5) DEER
(6) HARE (7) WOLF (8) STOAT (9) HORSE
(10) CAMEL (11) OTTER (12) RABBIT
(13) DONKEY (14) WEASEL (15) BADGER
(16) LEOPARD (17) PANTHER (18) GORILLA
(19) ANTELOPE (20) ELEPHANT

Page 18

Across
(1) annoyed
(5) about
(6) amazing
(9) leapt
(11) glee
(12) sound

Down
(1) arrived
(2) nearly
(3) nag
(4) got
(7) glad
(8) mend
(10) too

Page 19

(1) pest, (2) reap, (3) hear, (4) shore,
(5) low, (6) foal, (7) blow, (8) bleat,
(9) palm, (10) ten

Page 20

(1) CANE (2) CANAL (3) CANDY (4) CANOE
(5) CANARY (6) CANDLE (7) CANNON (8) CANTER
(9) CANCEL (10) CANTEEN (11) MARK (12) MARE
(13) MARCH (14) MARRY (15) MARSH
(16) MARBLE (17) MARGIN (18) MARIGOLD
(19) MARGARINE (20) MARMALADE

Page 21

(1) duke, (2) club, (3) mule, (4) cub,
(5) costume, (6) tube, (7) tune, (8) tub,
(9) cube

Page 24

Across
(1) start
(3) surprise
(5) job
(6) big
(8) idea
(12) huge
(13) trick
(14) landed
(15) Pat

Down
(2) thought
(3) said
(4) sure
(7) pleased
(9) airport
(10) story
(11) simple

Page 25

(2) eleven, (3) three, (4) ten, (5) two,
(6) nine, (7) ten, (8) seven, (9) five,
(10) twenty

Page 26

(1) ARCH (2) WITCH (3) MATCH (4) CHAIR
(5) CHAIN (6) CHEESE (7) CHURCH (8) CRUTCH
(9) CHICKEN (10) CHERRIES

Page 27

(1) mushroom, (2) key, (3) clock, (4) bark

Page 28

crab	table	apple
octopus	chair	banana
fish	cupboard	lemon
candle	pistol	
torch	rifle	
light bulb	cannon	

Page 29

(2) gulp, (3) stab, (4) spot, (5) snap,
(6) spat, (7) rats, (8) snip, (9) stun,
(10) part, (11) snug, (12) lived

Page 30

(1) bald, (2) road, (3) lying, (4) rain